THE STORM

(The Tragedy of Sinai)

By

EUGENE HEIMLER

English Version (After the Hungarian)
and Introduction
by
Anthony Rudolf

THE STORM (THE TRAGEDY OF SINAI)

All inquiries in regard to performance etc. of this play to:

Anthony Rudolf
The Menard Press
8, The Oaks
Woodside Avenue
London N12 8AR
United Kingdom

Or to the publisher:
Miriam B. Heimler
P.O.Box 18422
Jerusalem 91183
Israel

Acknowledgement: One extract from the play has been previously
published in European Judaism No. 13, 1972-3, "Michael Goulston
Memorial Issue".

Published by:
The Eugene Heimler Literary Trust
Miriam Bracha Heimler (Trustee)
P.O.Box 18422
Jerusalem 91183
Israel

Cover photo: Istock no. 108330145; Jew lifting torah scroll
Cover design by Devorah Priampolsky

ISBN 978-0-9989593-1-3

Dr. Eugene Heimler's "THE STORM" is a powerful drama in verse that reveals the secret of the survival of the Jewish people and how the Jews have been able to overcome history's never-ending challenges.

The drama is rooted in the author's personal Nazi death-camp experiences and his ongoing meditation on the Jewish tragedy of Masada. It illuminates how societal barbarism enabled Romans, Christians and Nazis to avoid and deny personal responsibility for their hatred, cruelty and massacres. Yet, despite a history punctuated by atrocities, Heimler breathes hope into the future for Jews, by voicing God's affirmation of the eternity of their survival.

This masterpiece is particularly relevant today, as extremism, antisemitism and intolerance sweep like wild fire across university campuses as well as Western- and Middle Eastern societies. The timeless message of Dr. Heimler's deeply moving drama is needed now more than ever before, to penetrate souls and educate minds.

Eugene Heimler is a Holocaust survivor, world-renowned pioneer of Human Social Functioning, mentor, educator and bestselling author of

Night of the Mist -**"Best book ever written on the Holocaust"**
Dr. Sarah Fraiman-Morris, Professor of Holocaust Literature, Bar Ilan University

The Storm
"What began as a teenager's innocent, promising verse grew, through the nightmare of the Shoah, into a profound, mature human soul, plumbing the depths of history, philosophy and faith."
Rabbi Dr. André Ungar, New Jersey

"Eugene Heimler is A True Hero of the 20th Century"
Ronald A. Lewis, M.Ed.

Preface
By the Publisher

It is a great privilege, after more than forty years, to republish this timeless dramatic work by Dr. Eugene Heimler. Out of the ashes of Auschwitz himself, Heimler paints a multidimensional vision of Jewish history and in THE STORM powerfully illustrates to the reader that despite suffering, or rather because of it, man is not only able, with the help of God, to survive, but gives the message, "… AND BECAUSE STRENGTH IS ETERNAL LIKE THE SUN, I KNOW TODAY THERE IS NO DEATH."

Soaked with Judaism and Jewish history, Eugene Heimler lived his life under this motto and created a method, with which he helped thousands of hopeless, suffering fellow men to survive their own psychological challenges and to turn them into victory, just as the Jewish people have done throughout Jewish history.
How to overcome obstacles and to turn suffering and pain into opportunities to grow and use those very disadvantages for creativity was Heimler's life's work.

In THE STORM he interweaves time, ages and scenes in Jewish history into one message: The Jewish people live, by the grace of God, whatever the challenges.
On the cover of Heimler's original Hungarian manuscript he wrote in his powerfully determined handwriting: *"The past lives in the present and the present lives in the past".*

We owe the present poetic artistry of this English translation to Anthony Rudolf's penetrating rendition. Himself a poet, he spent many hours discussing with Eugene Heimler the intricacies and complexities of this major work and was thus able not only to translate this work from Hungarian into English, but to create an epic masterpiece.

The translator deserves unending appreciation and gratitude for his momentous accomplishment.

Miriam Bracha Heimler
Jerusalem, May 8, 2018

P.S.
Anthony Rudolf hopes in the future to revisit the translation and may want to make some revisions.
I have made some minor changes as to the expressions of the name of God in order to help readers understand the play better.

Introduction
by the Translator

Hungarian is not a language I am acquainted with, even superficially. Consequently, to put Eugene Heimler's verse drama into English, I needed a line-by-line crib. In this instance the line-by-line was not supplied as a package to be taken on faith, but was worked out by Heimler and myself. Only when we were satisfied that the line-by-line was as well constructed as such a hybrid machine can ever hope to be, could I begin to make my attempt at an acceptable English version on <u>The Storm</u>. Our battles having been fought, I was henceforth on my own. At last, with Heimler's blessing, I could permit myself to think in units longer than the line. In fact, the battles had resembled the ones that go on inside one's own head when translating from a language one knows well. At the same time, the give-and-take, the process of negotiation, between us, formed a privileged moment, an authentic and cherished I-Thou experience, in our friendship. I am told, by those who know, that the original is a landmark in contemporary Hungarian verse/drama. I hope I have done the work justice. Having been involved in both stages of this verse translation from a language I do not know, I must emphasize, even more strongly than is usually the case, that the responsibility for the outcome is 100 % mine.

Eugene Heimler has made a profound impact on psychiatric social work and related fields in Britain and elsewhere through his pioneering of Social Functioning. The years of struggle to develop the method while remaining true to the vision despite the constraints of reality are described in Heimler's books.

When the Nazis invaded Austria in 1938, Heimler was 16. Around that time he read Josephus Flavius on the Jewish War. And, in Heimler's own words, "I was loved then, perhaps for the first time; and to my friend and first wife-to-be, Eva, I spoke a great deal about my hope that one day I might be able to make sense of what happened in Masada and what was happening to us in the middle of the twentieth century". The Storm was written some thirty years later. It is rooted both in his experiences of the Holocaust and its ever-present aftermath and in his continuing meditation on the theme of Masada.

The drama begins in Masada, moves to Sinai and thence to Roman Palestine. From there it moves to a German city in the Middle Ages, to the Holocaust and finally to post-Holocaust Palestine and Israel.
Eleazar Ben-Yair, the leader of Masada, is almost always present. The play, needless to say, is not a naturalistic representation of historical events. It is a morality play making demands on the conscience as well as the consciousness of the reader or spectator, akin to, without having been influenced by, Brecht. The several replayings of a basic configuration or moment, the role of the Spirit, the symbolization, the use of verse, are all means – through "distancing" – of conveying a threefold message:
1) the psychological responsibility of the Church for the Holocaust of which Heimler is a survivor; 2) the individual's responsibility, within society, for using even his worst experiences in order to transcend them and make a better world. "Do not ask why pain – only what is to be done with it"; 3) the indestructibility of the human spirit.

While The Storm could not have been written without a profound commitment to Judaism, Judeity and Judaicity (I am using Albert Memmi's conceptual structure), to Jewish origin and destiny, it would not have the impact that it does have if it did not move from the particular to the general. The Jewish minority experience, especially of suffering, as articulated throughout the ages, has become emblematic. The matrix-event of our civilization is Auschwitz, or rather,

Auschwitz/Hiroshima. On our individual and collective response to that event hangs the fate of our civilization. If we do not hear the cries of the victims, we shall not deserve, shall not know how, to continue bearing the responsibility for ensuring that our divided and tormented planet may yet become a peaceable kingdom. "Only for the sake of the hopeless ones have we been given hope", wrote Walter Benjamin. Heimler's play is a cry from the heart of that minority of minorities, the few who returned from the house of the dead: the survivors of the death camps.

Anthony Rudolf
London, February 1976

To Eva

who died in Auschwitz, July 1944

CHARACTERS:
The Spirit

Flavius Silva
(Procurator of Rome, Roman soldier, Bishop, Pope)

Cerealius Vetiliamus
(The Tribune, Roman soldier, priest, Dominican priest)

Eleazar Ben-Yair
(Leader of Masada, Moses)

Yehoshua
(Jew, cobbler, kibbutznik)

Akiva
(Jew, poet, kibbutznik)

John
(Jew, rabbi, kibbutznik)

The Voice

Eleazar's daughter

Seven pagans:
Ephesus, Smyrna, Pergamum, Thyatira, Sardis, Philadelphia, Laodicea
(Crusader, members of SS)

Ephesus – General of a European nation
Smyrna – high ranking SS Officer
Philadelphia – hangman
Chorus of Jews, echo, **1st Jew, 2nd Jew**
Chorus of people.

PROLOGUE TO SCENE 1

Before the curtain rises, a man in dark clothes appears on stage. Only his face is visible, illumined in a milk-white circle of light.

SPIRIT   I have been asked to appear before you
                 not to explain, but to state
                 that what you are about to witness
                 is not a tale: I am dressed
                 this way on purpose
                 because a modern audience would not
                 recognize a spirit if it saw one.
                 My problem is that, very gently,
                 I have to let you know
                 that I am not what I appear to be.
                 You would not believe me anyway.

The curtain rises. He walks casually to the side of the stage and points towards Masada.

SPIRIT   When the Lord pinned the sun on the sky
                 and hurled eternal darkness into space,
                 when the moon and stars awoke to life,
                 He breathed into the world: I AM.
                 And grass and tree and lake and stone
                 reverberated with the heavenly sounds.
                 Beneath the distant sky the world
                 resounded, and every pebble
                 was throbbing with the pulse of life.
                 And as the brightness spread above the sea
                 I came forth from the abyss
                 of mystery. Then the Lord said:
                 My son, help me pour the message
                 into earthly moulds. Beyond the light,

3

fear is trembling. You must become
the strength, the way, the meaning.
Life on earth is still unconscious.
Seek a form that can contain awareness
and once you have found it show it to me
that I may breathe eternal life
into it. As I walked across
the void of the world one day I discovered
what appeared human within it. And then
the Eternal spoke: how small is the mind
of man, yet suffering will cause it
to be found. Those flames! It seems that man
is dead. But my spirit still lives
in their heart and mind. They cannot ever
be annihilated. No night
can destroy
the man God's spirit burns like a toy.
He will survive throughout the ages
until one day he understands my message.

SCENE 1

73 C.E. (A.D.) April 15th. Night.

Before the last battle. The tent of Flavius Silva, Procurator of
Rome. The torches of the Roman camp can be seen through
the opened flap at the back of the tent, and in the distance
Masada is seen burning. The wind at times appears to be
carrying the cries of slaves. On the left is the Dead Sea. It
mirrors back the moon and all the fires.

When the curtain rises, Flavius Silva is alone at the entrance
of the tent. He is looking at the burning mountain and
listening to the noises of the night. After a few minutes, the
Tribune, Cerealius Vetiliamus, appears before the tent. He

gives the Roman salute. At first, being preoccupied, Silva
does not notice him. Then he sees Vetiliamus.

SILVA

Everything here is alien
Vetiliamus. Only
The rays of known stars
connect me still to Rome.
Do you hear the wind's cries?
Everything is dead. We
are a dead world's guardians.

VETILIAMUS

The last night is
very long, always.

SILVA

Spasms of loneliness flower
over the desert, and from the Dead Sea
shadows rise for their restless journey.

VETILIAMUS

Three years I've been watching
that mountain peek and cursing
the moment that brought me here.
I sometimes felt that time
had met its death. No past,
no present, no future, no battle,
no peace, nothing exists,
only that mountain peak and
a great emptiness everywhere.

SILVA

I am tired, Vetiliamus.
I was born to fight,
not to hang around.
I was born to conquer,
not to wait. Months
crawled like grains of sand
dribbling away. All passed
in total monotony.

5

It does not matter whether
there is fighting or even victory.

VETILIAMUS   Last night I wandered the streets
of Rome. Beneath the columns
of the Elysian fields I sought
my lover's burning lips. Desire
raised me
to unknown, godly heights.
The kiss was sweet under
the sky of Rome, and the desire
was sweet that played the music
I was still a man.
And then I was sitting
in the great amphitheatre and
I was watching the famous Hebrew,
Demetrius Liban, play
"The Apollonian Jew". I watched
the approving Roman faces and
applause, like a hurricane, tore
the Roman sky. Then
I awoke and the Judean wind
jeered in my face. We lie
in a barren desert's womb
while the Jews in Rome live
like victors and free men.
We are nothing but slaves.
While they are embracing their women
in cushioned beds
we are embracing the hot
sands. We shall probably die
and the emperor sleeps on the naked
breasts of his Jewish mistress
and has no thought
for the existence of Masada.

SILVA   I too learned hate in
                 this gloomy place. Until now
                 only contempt nestled
                 in my heart. A soldier
                 restores order, and then
                 moves on. But you are right,
                 Vetiliamus, even
                 if we win, there will be
                 no victory.

VETILIAMUS   Their temple lies in ruins;
                 at dawn Masada will be
                 as dead as burned shards.
                 But everywhere the Jews live on.

SILVA   I fear the way I hate,
                 Vetiliamus. And through
                 my fear, I bear my hatred.

VETILIAMUS   The slaves pray at dawn, at dusk.
                 Whip and curse are in vain.
                 They turn their broken bodies
                 to Jerusalem, to their temple, that heap
                 of rubble. Beyond the vanquished
                 stone lives their God
                 hovering invisible over
                 Judaea. What is eternal,
                 Rome will never destroy.
                 What the fathers whisper into
                 the ears of their sons is what
                 they shout at the soldiers who curse
                 them.

SILVA   Such defiance is dangerous
                 for courage lurks beyond
                 their madness. Courage made

Rome great, and the courage
of slaves is endangering Rome.

VETILIAMUS   Yes, at first the officers
whispered to each other
there is strength behind this courage.
And then like the gaping mouth
of a whirlpool, it began
to suck our soldiers in.
In Jerusalem they killed each other
before we came and then
fought us like wild beasts.
I still remember their priests
who prayed
until the last moment,
oblivious of death.
I see one solution only,
Sir, wipe out
all traces of them and their memory.

SILVA   I am an ordinary man, Vetiliamus.
When I am happy, I fall
into joy's silken folds.
When I am sad, I feel
the weight of passing years.
When love invades me
lilies of the valley
flower in my body.
When I hate, I hate my hate.
I love what I know.
I love my country, Rome and
if necessary, would die for her.
If the emperor orders
"destroy them"
I would not hesitate
but if my own soul says

the same words, deep shame
snakes through me. Here
in the back of beyond
I am forced to think, and the thoughts
give me pain. I have learned
there are depths beyond
the meaning of human life
that follow me around
like ghosts. Vetiliamus,
tell me honestly,
on your Roman word,
could an invisible spirit live
within the rubble? Can it be
that in this barbarous desert
where no birds fly
under the burning sky,
the spirit of a living
God hovers?

VETILIAMUS   I do not know, Sir.

SILVA   Not knowing is
                  worse than knowing the worst.

VETILIAMUS   You see what they have done,
                  Procurator: they
                  have breathed into us
                  the disease of doubt
                  and taken away
                  from us the certainty of faith.

SILVA   And tomorrow when we have
                  destroyed the last wall standing
                  in the way of Rome
                  and annihilated
                  every living life in

Masada, the ruins will whisper
across the shadows of the long
years to come that kill, we did
yet there is no victory.

PROLOGUE TO SCENE 2

SPIRIT   What you are about to see are miracles
                          lighting across this dreadful night.
                          Beyond pain lives the light of hope
                          and beyond death I exist eternally.

                          As blind history dribbles away, your
                          eyes will see what my eyes now see.
                          And when pain drizzles blooded tears
                          do not forget there is no such thing
                          as death.

                          What wild ages raze to the ground
                          will live on as long as
                          the earth goes round.

SCENE 2

The curtain rises. A few hours later. The small synagogue in
Masada. Fire embraces everything outside. Men are praying.
Their shadows move restlessly, like giant ghosts. Only
Hebrew prayers can be heard, with intermittent cries. Outside
the synagogue, although they are not visible, the masses of
Masada stand and their presence is felt by their reaction to
prayers and noises. Eleazar Ben-Yair, the leader of Masada,
slowly comes to the front of the stage and addresses the
audience as if they are the invisible masses of Masada.

ELEAZAR

What the Law was never able
to accomplish – that we stand united
before the Eternal –
Rome has brought about
with a single legion. What our fate
had always denied us – that we
confront the meaning of our existence -
swirling death and flames
have now achieved.
We lived our lives in the noisy layers
of moments. The hours congealed
like putty.
The din blocked and deafened our ears.
Locked out, life's voice
cried before our houses.
And, color-blind,
our eyes stared into greyness.
And in the dead sunshine we,
specks of dust,
were swept into endless death.

The blooded rags have fallen
from our ears now.
Our eyes behold a new color –
death's dark incubus,
and across this great night
dawns the judgment of the Eternal.
The Roman whip is God's punishment
and now rains down
for the last time on
Israel's bleeding back.

Yet great and mighty nations
have been swept by tempests
off the face of the earth.
Pock-marked maps preserve

their scars.
We do not live only in space, and time
does not bind us to one nation alone.
Our home is the Law and the Idea.

(lifts up the Torah)

So long as these scrolls remain alive
in the deepest recesses of living souls
here and in Egypt, in Rome and
in Babylon, the people of Israel shall
bring forth fruit,
wherever the Law survives.

But now, in this night, we must decide
before dawn's blood drips
from the sky,
what death we wish for ourselves:
the death of the slave
or the death of free men?
What is nobler: to surrender and perish
by the savage's hand, or to kill mother,
loved one and child? Time is
tightening. You have to decide.

YEHOSHUA   Does it matter how a man dies?
Afraid, trembling, proud or defiant?
Earth's womb knows little difference.
Let us send envoys to Flavius Silva,
bearing the message "Sir, have mercy!"
and hope that many hundreds
remain alive.

AKIVA   Ignoble and cowardly words!
People who look to Rome for mercy
deserve a thousand deaths.

Where was the mercy in Caesarea
when on the Sabbath they tore the flesh
of our mothers and children?
In Damascus the blood ran high in the
streets between the stone house,
like storm-swelled rivers.

YEHOSHUA   But rumor says Silva is humane.

AKIVA   The son of a Roman mother born
under the Roman sky, remains a wolf
even when dressed in the skin of a
lamb.

ELEAZAR   My brothers, why do we torture
each other's souls even
at this moment of disaster?

YEHOSHUA   It is easy to speak, at the end
of one's life.
But hard is the fate of those who are
young. What have I seen of the
pulsating world but smoke, fire and
charred ruins?
The mirage of desire has not called me
to a woman yet. I have only tomorrow
because I have no yesterday.
I am not a coward, only young.

AKIVA   Forgive the wounding arrows of my
words. At times age does not know
what it is saying. You dream of the
miracles of flesh. But that flame fled
my blood long ago.
And because my senile brain
has forgotten the fever that once

13

embraced me, I perceive
as eternal, eternal decay. The great
loneliness of fear has sneaked
into the place of desire and I hide
my cowardice behind a mask of
courage.

JOHN

Young or old,
we must come to our decision now,
in this fort, while we are still free:
what will our death mean for those
who survive?
On the other side of this fortress,
across the Judean hills,
even the slavery life will go on
as before. And slavery, like life,
is not eternal. Our deaths will live
in those who seek hope at a new dawn.
And this is the message of our death
for the ears of tyrants:
"Beware – one day the persecuted
will rise from the dust and their
broken chains falling to earth like seed,
will make the sun-soaked morrow
fertile.
Beware, for the whip
lashes the heavenly spirits and
from the river of tears a mighty ocean
comes to sweep away all persecutors".
Our death will have meaning, and one
day here, will sing to the world:
Masada lives and will live forever.

ELEAZAR

Brothers, now you have to decide.

CHORUS

(within and without)

14

We free men,
at the top
of this mountain,
before the past,
before the future,
thus we swear:
father, kill
the fruit of your loin.
Husband, mortally
wound your wife.
Brother, put your
Brother to sleep.
Friend, put out
the burning light
of your friend
and fire shall burn
every remnant
of Masada,
and ruins shall
declare to slaves
wherever they
may be that
freely we placed
the restless great
weight of our souls
into the hands
of the Eternal.

There are some who cry, some who stare into nothingness,
but gradually everyone except Eleazar leaves the synagogue.
When Eleazar is alone, he falls to his knees and, surrounded
by the fire outside, desperately raises his arms.

ELEAZAR   Man's knowledge is so tiny,
and his lack of knowledge is endless,
like the sea.

15

Why must we bleed for our ignorance,
suffer pain for every grain of truth?
Must we plunge our swords
into living flesh for our memory
to survive beneath the burning sky?
Why death of tiny writhing children,
what is the reason for their fate?
I fail to understand Your cruel,
bitter law, the foggy intentions
of Your ways.
All I know is we live and die
searching for meaning
in the jungle of the world.

From everywhere can be heard the shrieks and pain of death.
The night is full of it. While this is going on, he covers his
ears and almost obsessionally shouts.

ELEAZAR   You my Eternal God,
                   entered into a covenant
                   with Abraham on Mount Moriah
                   and forbade forever
                   human sacrifice. You formed a nation
                   from Isaac's loin and
                   took us from slavery to Mount Sinai.

The scene changes to the light at the top of Mount Sinai. And
Eleazar watches these changes with consternation and fear.

ELEAZAR   Oh Eternal God, I have been staring
                   into a mirror of solitude for forty
                   days and nights.
                   I saw the roaring whirlpool of my lust,
                   dark tentacles chaining me to earth,
                   and nameless monsters.
                   Life had no meaning.

16

I drifted pleasantly in the waters
like a leaf that has not yet been
washed clean of its original colors.
I was not fertile from Your light.
Denying You – I denied myself.
I fall now, pierced by a thousand
terrors, before You, my God.
Orgies of memory clamor in my brain
and dimly form the thought
that You alone are the beginning and
the destiny of everything;
dimly form the thought that I have
hidden You beneath a layer of fear,
because You lived in me like life lives
in the coldness of stones.

Eternal God, my Lord, how strange
is the taste upon my tongue now.
How strange is the light in my eyes
and strange the hues of my mind.
Damp arms of fear reach out for me
to embrace, and these words echo
strangely over the dead and cursed
emptiness.
Oh God, I, the man, cry to You.
Allow me to come to You, allow me
to see You. I implore You, let me see
life's real colors with my blind eyes.
Let me fall into Your eternal time.
Allow my soul to be blessed
in Your time.
For You know too well the ways of
insignificant man,
You are beyond his words and gestures
and You see deeply that we are not
what we make ourselves out to be.

17

My God, terrorized with giddiness,
I spin towards You. My words dry up.
My tongue is parched. In my innermost
brain lights flash. Speak to me,
my God.

ECHO   Speak to me, my God.

ELEAZAR   I once watched the slaves,
                         and their masters.
                         My heart was full of pity
                         because slave-owners themselves
                         are slaves and in the heart of slaves
                         burns freedom.
                         There is no certainty anywhere.
                         Storms are playing, as far as the eye
                         can see, with the dust of human beings.
                         Everywhere are empty crevices.
                         And the soul cries out for nourishment
                         in the enormous desert.
                         Only You can be that certainty,
                         my God.
                         There is no anchor in the outside
                         world. You are the cause, the reason,
                         the sense of every living thing.
                         Speak to me, my God.

ECHO   Speak to me, my God.

ELEAZAR   My mind is whirling in two
                         dimensions.
                         I am different here on Sinai
                         than I really am. And at Masada's
                         dawn I shall turn into a different man,
                         a dead man. Who am I, oh God,
                         and in what time have You placed

Your servant?

Suddenly the silence becomes frightening to him. Earth and
heaven are still. Suddenly lightning and thunder pierce the
night, and all the colors of the spectrum fill the stage. The
voice floods the theatre.

VOICE   There are no past and present in the
                   book of destiny. They only seek, who
                   have no time. The sky and earth live
                   in your heart. Death and life together
                   are the truth like two sides of a coin.
                   Uncertainty is your only certitude.
                   There are no solutions within
                   the bond of flesh.
                   But pain and joy will teach you
                   the great secret that lives within
                   your heart.
                   Teach thousands who, like falling stars,
                   shine only as they fall in space.
                   The Idea whose meaning escapes you
                   will be your strength in the long nights.
                   Now I take you across humility
                   and the trembling of the broken,
                   across the hate all around
                   like the icy space surrounding
                   your world. I take you across meaning
                   and meaninglessness because I chose
                   you for pain so that you shall form
                   meaning out of it.
                   Do not ask why pain,
                   only what is to be done with it.

ELEAZAR   The burden You placed on our
                   shoulders is so heavy,
                   we collapse beneath its weight.

19

We are only insignificant vermin
and our humanity is as distant
as the sky.
What is the Law worth, if we cannot
perceive its meaning?
What is the radiance of life worth
if our eyes only perceive a
night of mist?
Eternal God, behold the dirty rags
of dawn crawl slowly above the
sea of death.
Your people will be no more
by sunrise.
What Law is worth this awful
deadly fate?
So much barren human sacrifice.
So much biting pain. The torch of Law
You gave to light our way will
burn us dead
because there is no path to tread.

As the voice begins to speak Eleazar prostrates himself.

VOICE   Step out of time and return to
                               your todays before life's spark fades
                               into endless night. Complete your
                               voyage across the somber years
                               and you will find answers to your
                               human plight.

Back to Masada. In the synagogue, Eleazar is still kneeling.
And the screams of the Jews killing each other fill the stage.

PROLOGUE TO SCENE 3

SPIRIT

Power is immune to violence
and only gives new strength to the man
who is suffering. Do not allow
death to lead you astray
as he swoops upon the crosses.
Do not allow the flowing blood
to confuse you, for it is the carrier
of the soul. Only a man
possessed by live demons believes
nothing but slaughter is eternal.
They think that this is all:
life, death, pleasure, pain.
With his weapons, he who digs graves
knows nothing of the coming
reawakening.

SCENE 3

A few years later. Late afternoon. Dusk on the Judean Hills.
The sun's rays fall onto two crosses. On one, Eleazar is
dying. On the other is his daughter. Two Roman soldiers
(Silva and Vetiliamus) stand guard, and three Jews stand or
kneel around the crosses. The characters are as before.
Vetiliamus turns towards Eleazar and his daughter.

VETILIAMUS

These wretched rebels,
will they never die?

SILVA

I do not know who is
living, who dying.
Everything is a nightmare
from which there will never
be awakening.

21

YEHOSHUA	Sir, find mercy in your heart and save them while you can.
SILVA	The right of pardon is not within my powers. I only obey orders.
YEHOSHUA	If the humanity in your heart is not victorious, millions will kill in the future – repeating the words: I only obey orders. My Lord, the Law of mercy is higher than that of man.
SILVA	What becomes of the order of things if I weaken? What becomes of Rome if rebels remain alive?
VETILIAMUS	Rome is more important than our hearts' humanity.
YEHOSHUA	What is order when it is blind to mercy? What strength knows no weakness?
VETILIAMUS	It is the right of the strong to break the weak.
AKIVA	Do not implore them and do not weep. Only remember, across the millennia, force is never convinced by tears. only by a greater force.
VETILIAMUS	Behold, Silva, the Jew now speaks the truth.

22

AKIVA   (to Yehoshua)
                 Remember the dying
                 morning, noon and evening,
                 and one day, when the Roman bleeds
                 on the cross, remember what they
                 taught us: the right of the strong
                 is to break the weak.

JOHN   What pagan words are these,
                 Akiva? We cannot become our own
                 enemies and act like Romans.

AKIVA   Why should we be different
                 from others? Why should we bleed
                 for those murders?

JOHN   Oh I myself often feel
                 the burden of truth of your words.
                 I too would like at times
                 to shake the message of Sinai
                 from me, but that is impossible.
                 The very thought fills me with shame.

Eleazar turns to his daughter, from one cross to the other.

ELEAZAR   Who are you, girl? I know you.

GIRL   Out of a dream I was born,
                 I am yours. I am your blood,
                 your companion under the setting sun.

ELEAZAR   Crucifixion has dulled my brain.
                 Help me on my heavy path
                 and tell me, girl,
                 what brought us to this hill of pain?

Akiva, John and Yehoshua are praying, swaying in the traditional manner. Silva and Vetiliamus, bored, look at the crucified.

GIRL   My father, we have sinned.
        Murder and mortal fear surround us.
        It is criminal. Our country was
        destroyed by brute force and savages.
        And the Law fell into nothingness.
        Yet this cannot be the end
        of everything. This curse will be
        the beginning of a blessing.
        I am here, born to restore your
        Messianic dream.

Suddenly seven pagans appear on the stage. They represent seven Greek cities.

EPHESUS   (to Silva)
        We come in the name of Rome
        to take these rebels.
        Here is a message from the emperor.

Silva reads the scroll, and having read it carefully, says:

SILVA   Yes, the rebels are yours.
        Do what you will.

The pagans kill the three Jews while the Romans stand there without caring.

SILVA   Come Vetiliamus, our tasks
        are at an end. I wonder
        where our blind fate
        will lead us now.

24

The two Romans leave the stage.

GIRL   (to father)
        My God, what now, beneath the
        crosses, seven pagans staring,
        ready to pounce. Their starved eyes
        clamp on my flesh like shameless flies
        upon the flesh of fruit.
        Father, father, fear's vast hurricane
        engulfs my womb. We are crucified
        and they are seven…

EPHESUS   Old man Jew,
        we take your daughter now,
        for like the sun her beauty blinds.

SMIRNA   Her white skin
        is soft like fresh bread
        and we are mighty hungry, Jew.

PERGAMUM   Her breasts
        are like the hills of Galilee,
        tempting us to climb them.

THYATIRA   Between her thighs
        her secret hides and we shall force
        the secret open.

SARDIS   In her oasis
        God resides and we want to see
        this hidden God.

PHILADELPHIA Her lips
        like blood-red cherries, summon
        our thirsty tongues to a feast.

LAODICEA   We shall kill you now,
                  you bloody Jew. But your daughter
                  will live with us.

GIRL   Father, father,
                  do not let them take me!

ELEAZAR   Words I hear but my mind is deaf.
                  What is this howling chaos?
                  I am no one.
                  I am so tired.

With a hammer they release the girl from the cross and tear
off her clothes. They dance around and eventually push her
down and rape her bleeding body in turn while the others
continue dancing. This episode is a total degradation of
sexuality.

CHORUS OF
PAGANS   (while raping)
                  Your father is
                  finished. Open
                  the secret of
                  your flesh. Your
                  bastard son
                  will deny the dream
                  of your ancestors.
                  We shall teach him
                  to hate, to lie, to
                  betray. Thus do
                  we take revenge
                  on you for giving
                  an impossible Law,
                  an invisible God
                  to the world.

26

Eleazar turns his dying eyes upwards. One of the pagans in the advancing night stabs Eleazar with his spear while the others drag the girl off-stage.

PROLOGUE TO SCENE 4

SPIRIT

Only the scenery changes.
The actors are always the same.
It matters little whether hatred wears
this garment or some other cloak.
Yet transcending every hate
my spirit stirs within them now.
Preacher, poet, cobbler - look
for meaning beneath the sun.
As the sands of time run down
slowly men will come to know me.
I shall not always stand aloof,
apart from them, before this curtain.

SCENE 4

Some time in the Middle Ages. The synagogue in a small German town. Outside, through the windows, the light of fire and shadows. Apparently the crusaders are trying to break through the city walls. When the curtain rises figures are swaying in prayer, as in the Masada synagogue scene, and on the wall the shadows are magnified like ghosts. In detail and atmosphere everything is almost identical with that of the synagogue in Masada. Eleazar walks to the front of the stage and speaks to the audience.

ELEAZAR

Once you were with me in the blooded
depths of the night's darkness.

You died and then you were reborn.
Now death beckons you again.
You were with me in Masada
when the sword of Rome
swished through the night
and on the top of the hills when
the Roman hammer
 nailed you to the cross.
Now you sit here in a different time.
Only your dress
is different from before.
But the burdens
are just the same.
Outside this synagogue
force, naked force, makes an orgy
in the great world,
and across the borders
millions are frightened
for their tender lives.
Powerful men still have the power
and in the weak are flames
of trembling hunger.

The crusaders are coming.
They have inherited Rome
in the base world's midnight
and we still proclaim the ancient laws.
Once, long ago, we debated
Whether there was purpose
in our death for those
who live on, and today we
are living. We believe in life.
And the meaning of life is knowledge.
Its message must be absorbed.
This is why across the bloody centuries
we still study the Law. Akiva,

you are a poet, tell us what
you have learned.
John, you are one of our teachers.
What is history's secret message?
Yehoshua, you are a shoemaker.
What did your craft teach you?

For a few seconds there is silence and Akiva, the eldest of the
three, comes slowly to the front of the stage.

AKIVA   In the night's endless silence
                           when dreams descend on weary eyelids
                           we step into a world that is eternal,
                           hovering beyond the known order.
                           The heart only is capable
                           of this strange journey,
                           and without dreams consciousness
                           is death
                           because without secrets there is no
                           recognition.
                           And I, the poet, now declare to you
                           the place my words' music comes from
                           is beyond everything we know.
                           And if I write down the melody I hear,
                           I am only a harp in the fingers of God.
                           Those who write, create music, paint
                           or carve, all know the depth of the
                           dreams whence all strength springs.
                           And because strength is eternal
                           like the sun I know today
                           there is no death.

ELEAZAR   And what is your answer to those
                           whom dreams avoid
                           as the sun avoids the night,

who only believe what their eyes see
and deny the world beyond?

AKIVA   We all feel the caressing sun's
rays, and the wind like loving women
caresses the tired brow. We all
feel the opening of our children's
world and the love which like a secret
thread binds human hearts together.
We feel the pleasant pains of love,
and the living mystery between
the thighs of women,
and at a tired dawn
the dawning knowledge
that God resides beyond all pleasure.
We all see the buds of trees,
and at a spring dusk clouds
dispersing on the sky's
blue mirror, clouds which
like lovers chase each other
until they finally embrace.
We see our mother's face
on a beautiful morning
and her mild smile which remains
with us for good.
We see valleys and mountains
and tiny lakes between the thighs
of hills.
Eleazar, one need not be a dreamer
to dream. The eye sees only the forms,
but without the heart there is
no content anywhere.
If we see only what exists,
we see nothing
because things are in constant change.
Our only certainty is change.

And if our brain is deaf to the dream
it suffocates the heart of things.

He walks back to his seat and John the rabbi comes to the
front of the stage.

JOHN
      The sea of suffering is icy cold.
      And the stream in its depth
      finds its way blindly.
      If we do not know which way is
      the shore, it is only too easy to give
      up the fight. Why these blind forces
      are sweeping us, we will never
      understand.
      But what use to the drowning man
      to know the reason for his pain?
      The only question that needs an answer
      now is whether we have the strength to
      swim towards the shore.
      If we do not complain about the past
      but clearly perceive where our future
      lies, beyond the shore our ancient land
      is waiting, cities and fields,
      mountains and rivers,
      labor, love and life.
      Sunsets are waiting
      on the banks of the Jordan
      and new dawns beneath
      the mountain of God.
      Living hopes of all the dead
      await us beneath the cinders
      of Jerusalem.
      The teacher's task is, always,
      to learn and to share with others
      his scanty knowledge.
      This is what I have learned,

31

and give to you in this fateful night
pregnant with mighty flames.

Goes back to his seat. Yehoshua waits till he sits down and
comes to the front of the stage.

YEHOSHUA   First you take the leather.
                   Then the knife. The knife shapes the
                   skin. The feet outlined – how long?
                   How high? Then with tiny nails
                   the master joins the uppers and
                   the soles.
                   Now all of you listen:
                   The skin is dead, and so is the heart.
                   And the nails lie dead, inert,
                   because the image is in the mind
                   of the master. He sees the shoe,
                   as yet unmade, because creation
                   dreams in the master's soul. You see,
                   he sees what none of you can see:
                   the silent wait of toiling hours
                   while his hands give shape
                   to dead matter.
                   In his hands the matter is transformed
                   into new form: and the shoe is ready.
                   Without the master, is no creation.
                   And without the hunter
                   who brings the leather
                   the master is nothing. You have
                   to sweat for knowledge, and there is
                   no trade without patience.
                   There is pride in the well-made shoe,
                   which matches the poet's inspiration.
                   Sometimes sitting on my low round
                   cobbler's stool,
                   inhaling deep the fragrance of the skin

I think perhaps we too are such shoes
in the hand of God.
And who understands the craftsman
better than God who does the same
with His human material?

Goes back to his seat. Sits down. Eleazar speaks to the
audience while off-stage a shouting mob is heard.

ELEAZAR   Perhaps you think we've gone mad:
to talk of life in the hour of death.
That we ought to plan
to save our lives.
But defense we learned stems from
truth and knowledge and both as yet
are like a helpless child.
What we know is like green fruit,
unripe.
Every beast fights
but the right of man is to learn
and learn.

First Jew runs into the synagogue.

1ST JEW   The bishop has opened the city gates.
The mob is killing everything
that comes its way.
They come like a flood. This is the end.

ELEAZAR   (as if he has heard nothing)
To live for knowledge
is the only purpose.
To die for that purpose
is the only meaning.
Those who want to die, will die.

33

But I still cry
life.

Nobody moves. The second Jew runs into the synagogue.

2ND JEW   (out of breath)
                    The bishop, the bishop is on his way.
                    The crusaders have surrounded us.

The bishop (Silva) and the priest (Vetiliamus) enter the
synagogue. The bishop holds a crucifix, the priest a container
of holy water. Outside the roaring of a mob is heard.

BISHOP   (to Eleazar)
                    I come to you in the name
                    of Jesus to save your souls
                    at this hour
                    of despair. Whoever
                    allows his soul
                    to be redeemed will live
                    a free man in our midst.
                    But the fate of him who still
                    denies our Christ will be
                    pain and death. I come to
                    you in the name of Jesus.

ELEAZAR   Out in the street howls the mob,
                    human beasts thirsting for our blood.
                    What kind of goddamned
                    bloody church tolerates such things
                    and mouths redemption
                    in the shade of death?

BISHOP   I am not responsible
                    for the mob.
                    I repose no faith

in savage power
but I cannot lower the dam
to hold back the sweeping
flood of crusaders.

Because you denied the word
of our Lord and because you nailed
our Jesus on the cross
no punishment can ever
be enough. Yet whoever
falls on his knees
and lets the holy water
touch his heathen brow
will gain freedom
unknown till now.
On your knees, you sinners,
while there is still time.

ELEAZAR   All we have left is our faith.
                   If it depart, we are truly dead.
                   This faith of ours
                   has whispered across long centuries
                   that God has no flesh or form,
                   no kin – father, mother or son.
                   What cannot be conceived
                   cannot be molded into form.
                   We cannot be killers of God because
                   you cannot kill what is unkillable.
                   Only pagans seek God in human form.
                   Only pagans kill in the name
                   of such gods.

PRIEST   Blasphemy, my lord in Christ.
                   There is no sense in saving
                   vermin like these. Satan
                   understands one thing:

fire consumes
their horrible flesh.

BISHOP

Vetiliamus, we are only men.
Satan lives in
everybody's heart.
If we do not forgive
these base deniers
we will never
receive absolution.
(to Eleazar)
On my knees I beg you:
In God's name, save your souls.

Nobody moves.

I do not desire
the sacrifice of death
and dying for false
ideals is vain.

AKIVA

And barren is the naivety
that a gesture and a drop of water
can liberate a man. And dangerous
the self-delusion that speaks of pardon
while the mob out there roars hate.

PRIEST

You bloody Jew.
Off-spring of the curse.
Your fate is death,
flames and agony.
Enough of your preaching.
Your worthless life
meets its fate at last.

The priest grabs the cross from the bishop's hand and strikes
Akiva with it. Then he runs to the door, tears it open and the
crusaders run into the synagogue. The crusaders are the very

same seven pagans as in the previous scene. The bishop falls
to his knees, praying.

PRIEST   Kill them. Drink
                              their blood: Tear
                              their ugly flesh apart.
                              Blind them: Cut out
                              their tongues in the name
                              of our Lord Jesus Christ.

The priest takes hold of Yehoshua and violently pushes his
head into the holy water, making the sign of the cross over
the drowning man. When the priest is sure he is dead, he
speaks.

PRIEST   The Lord has taken
                              His repentant child.

Ghastly slaughter is enacted in the synagogue. The Jews are
dragged out one by one, alive or dead, by the crusaders.
Blazing stakes are seen outside. The priest accompanies them
on their errands of murder, having placed the crucifix in front
of the ark of the covenant. Only the bishop remains in the
synagogue kneeling in front of the ark and the cross. A
solitary candle flickers in the darkness. Outside, the fires are
spreading and screams filter into the synagogue. Suddenly the
girl stands in front of the ark.

GIRL   General Silva,
                              hangman of Rome, bishop
                              of the church, do you remember
                              how things began?

BISHOP   (terrified)
                              Something glimmers
                              from a distant dream

	as if shadows are whispering dead words to me.
GIRL	The dreams' distance is the truth of yesterday. And the echo of the shadows resounds with your own words from the past. Because, General Silva, hangman and prince of the church, you were the servant of might. Until you master those mighty forces, you will be a tool in the thick, sticky nether world's grasp.
BISHOP	I do not know you, apparition. I do not know what you want of me.
GIRL	When man strays into truth's spell-binding circle he begins to deny the words of his own feelings. Do not deny me, Flavius Silva. If you do, hope is abandoned.
BISHOP	But if I do, what will become of my church?
GIRL	Yesterday you said: "What will become of Rome if I weaken?"
BISHOP	I remember nothing, and you, apparition, are a stranger to me.
GIRL	You had me killed on the cross.

38

You will kill me again.

BISHOP   Oh my Lord Jesus,
             save me from this ghost,
             stop up my ears lest I hear
             the voices of yesterday.

GIRL   You poor, poor feeble man,
             subservient to might,
             that might which scorns all weakness.

BISHOP   Away from this cursed place
             where Satan lives.

The bishop runs out of the synagogue and leaves the girl
standing alone in front of the ark and the cross in the weak
candlelight. Outside the fires have died out and there is
complete silence.

PROLOGUE TO SCENE 5

SPIRIT   Being a spirit is sometimes too hard
             when the long knife cuts right through
             the heart.
             I have come to this century, inferno
             of all ages on the earth. We now cross
             the ocean of the ages.
             They are a searching people,
             I am the spirit.
             I shall become a part
             of the flow of blood that courses
             strongly still through their arteries.
             When life is put out like a lamp
             I still live on
             beyond the blood. At times

millions of deaths
are nothing but the start of a
new life.

SCENE 5

Mediaeval courtroom. The Pope, Silva, is seated on a high
throne, wearing a papal crown, surrounded by pomp. The
accusers sit together in a separate box, side by side.
Vetiliamus is a Dominican priest, Ephesus the general of a
European nation, Smyrna a high-ranking SS officer with a
swastika on his arm-band. Sitting on the bench of the accused
are Eleazar, Akiva, John and Yehoshua.

A torture-rack, heavy with irons and hob-nails stands
perpendicular, awaiting the prisoners. Philadelphia wears the
dark uniform of a hangman with a hooded mask over his face.
As in the previous scene, the voices and shouts of the mob are
to be heard from beyond the windows, and through the
window, burning stakes can be seen, and later the belching
chimneys of the crematoria. The spirit and the girl too are on
the bench of the defenders. A few more pagans are seated
among the spectators.

For a few moments after the curtain goes up, all actors are
immobile, like stone statues. The prisoners wear the prison
uniform of the concentration camp. The pope makes the sign
of the cross over himself and stands before the throne.

POPE   In the name of the father,
                        son and holy ghost,
                        we have convened the court
                        of all the ages
                        to search out the vile
                        deeds of the accused.

40

We represent all times,
and the whole world.
History awaits our judgement.
You who accuse
must enact with dignity
the noble task
of bringing accusation.

(The pope makes the sign of the cross
over the accused and speaks to them.)

We
God's earthly deputy,
hereby ensure your right
of free defense.
If the pain of the rack
grows unbearable
just signal,
and your torture will abate.
For at this trial, -
suffer though you must,
we, in this chair, desire
only the truth,
not necessarily
your death. We desire
the truth in the name
of our Lord Jesus Christ.

(Once more he makes the sign of the
cross over himself)

Who is the first accuser now?

DOMINICAN   In the name of the holy church
I will accuse,
my holy father.

POPE   Peace unto you, Vetiliamus,
                        our faithful son.
                        But you may not charge them
                        in the name of the church.
                        Christ's church is neutral.
                        But you may lawfully bring
                        accusation on behalf of
                        the Dominican order.

DOMINICAN   (bows towards the pope)
                        So be it, father.
                        In the name of the priesthood
                        shall I now bring my charge?

POPE   And what is the charge,
                        our son, Vetiliamus?

DOMINICAN   (to the accused)
                        You have denied
                        that the Messiah has come. You still
                        await the miracle
                        that has already happened.

At the pope's signal the four prisoners are nailed to the rack.

POPE   (to the prisoners)
                        Answer the charge: who
                        speaks for the accused?

ELEAZAR   (points his finger at the Dominican)
                        He speaks of the miracle
                        of the Messiah.
                        What kind of miracle brought us here?
                        What salvation of the world
                        ever swelled with pain?

This is the midnight of the ages
and no one here raises his voice for us.

SPIRIT   Do not say that no one speaks:
         I shall remain with you.

ELEAZAR   Spirit of God, who would understand
         Your words in such a courtroom?

SPIRIT   You Eleazar, grasp the meaning
         of My words.

ELEAZAR   They
         are deaf. What good if
         I
         understand? We talk
         but they only hear what
         they want to hear.

GIRL   As we were together on the mountain
         so I am with you now, father,
         in your pain.

ELEAZAR   Girl, you are too young to fight them.
         Beware lest on a new cross
         you too be crucified again.

POPE   (to Eleazar)
         Well may your guilt and pain
         make you delirious, yet
         you must give an answer now.

ELEAZAR   You seek our denial, for
         your own Lord of doubt torments you
         beyond endurance. We are

your distorting mirror, reflecting
what lurks within the shadows of
your souls. You know there is no
salvation while wars rage
beneath their palls of smoke
and the hungry flames of madness
bite into the blue sky with their
fiery fangs. This trial is not staged
against ourselves
but against the devil that
lives within you.
Yet when all is said and done
it is we and not Satan who must die.

SPIRIT   Eleazar, resist, never weaken. He
                  who bears the spirit in his soul
                  is immortal.

ELEAZAR   But flesh surrounds the spirit.
                  Fragile flesh as thin as glass.
                  I shall speak as long as my flesh
                  permits.

DOMINICAN   Holy father, the accused
                  does not respond. He mumbles
                  words bereft of sense.

POPE   Suffering and guilt
                  have taxed his brain too hard.
                  Hangman, relax the ropes.

The hangman relaxes the strangling ropes on Eleazar's throat.

POPE   Address the other now, Vetiliamus.
                  What else does your indictment say?

44

DOMINICAN	(to John) You accepted Jesus as your Lord, but secretly remained a Jew, like the rest.
JOHN	(to girl) Once I knelt on the mountain height while savage forces killed your father. But I kept my faith with the truth you declared, and that truth is free like a bird and cannot be confined in a cage. If Rome had never sent the pagans to violate your gentle limbs, there would be no church no pope, no accusation, no rack, no pain, no vain defense, but the truth of Sinai: the water from the spring.
GIRL	Do not condemn these semi-humans who can adore the form and not the plan.
JOHN	But condemnation is within their power. What flows from me is human blood.
GIRL	Your flowing blood is your sacrifice as often seeds sprout from the dewy night.
POPE	Your babbling means you have denied the church.
JOHN	(in pain)

I deny whatever they claim is denial.

DOMINICAN   (to Yehoshua)
                 I baptized your father one
                 gory night to secure
                 your freedom among the sons
                 of men. Yet secretly
                 you denied Jesus Christ
                 and in stealth pursued
                 the faith of your forbears.

YEHOSHUA   Armed, you surrounded my father,
                 and forced his head
                 into the holy water.
                 I, the son have lived my life in fear.
                 If only I had lived my peoples faith
                 perhaps my soul would reach now
                 towards the sky.
                 But I sniveled for my life,
                 and betrayed our ancient truth
                 until this moment
                 when hated reality casts its awareness
                 into my dead soul.

                 Oh I was faithful to the church,
                 but now I am a dizzy leaf,
                 I seek the tree
                 whose fruit is my destiny.

DOMINICAN   These are my charges,
                 holy father. There is
                 no question
                 that the prisoners
                 have admitted them all.

POPE   Their sins are in no doubt now:

	but there are others in this court of law who will press charges in the wake of the priests.
GENERAL	I come here, holy father on the state's behalf.
POPE	What be the charges of state, General, my son?
GENERAL	Liberty reigns in our modern land. We gave a home to the homeless Jew. We tore off their yellow patch. Our laws offered equality for all. And soon they began to rise in science, commerce, and trade. Their names grew famous among men. Respect and trust surrounded their homes. The prisoners served as officers in the army, and were guardians of secret things. But they betrayed the Christian state and sold our secrets to the foe. I charge them with high treason and subversion, setting faithful nations against each other.
PEOPLE'S CHORUS	(outside)

You are the cause
of war. You kindle
the flame of hate.
Our sons are killed
because of you,
because you want
to rule our fate.

POPE

(to Akiva)
Now you may offer your defense.

AKIVA

Yes, we became
our countries' faithful sons
and the gentle rays of passing years
began to heal the gaping
wounds of flesh.
At first we still walked in fear,
then in time our spines grew straight
and we raised our heads like other men
and we, the homeless of the ages,
served our new land
with faithful pride.
Our ears forgot in time
the sounds of the past.
Our mothers taught us a new tongue
at a ruby dawn.
And a dream that, once,
we had our own land,
guttered like dying candles
beyond our imaginings. The religion
had become an empty frame
whence faith like wind had fled away.
We raced through
the Friday evening prayers
as if the dreadful past were only a tale.
Many of us frequented alien shrines

and betrayed the handful who sought
God in the ancient forms.
We mocked them,
disapproving their
outmoded ghetto ways
and we grew modern
in this modern world
as once before in the arms of Athens.
Yes we denied our forefathers' dreams
that the Judean hills await their sons.
When the state called us to fight
we marched to kill.
When the state demanded blood
we slit our veins.
When the state commanded: starve,
we pulled our belts even tighter,
and we ate when our country
told us we could.
Then one day the dead craters
erupted again.
The cruel lava scalded our homes.
valleys, mountains, seas
hissed we betrayed the fatherland,
the home.
And as the fire burned our future
to ashes
dazed we stared back into the
distant past:
the dead were weeping
on the banks of the Jordan
and thousands of memories
beckoned us home.

To nation and state
we have not been traitors
but to that ancient truth which

pushed us out
into the world, we have been.
Towards the state we are innocent
as babies in their mother's laps.
But we are guilty of betraying
our living past.

GENERAL   How touching are the tears
of the accused. I almost
weep with pity
as I hear them wail.
But beware. Speech
was always their most
cunning skill, cleverly
disguising brutal
facts. The state
must tear off this mask,
display the naked
hidden crimes
of these monsters
and demand that all
the heathen traitors
who offended law,
morality and nation
shall die a thousand deaths.

AKIVA   We are innocent. We are innocent.

SPIRIT   In vain you hope to offer some defense.
Those without reason search for none.
The world passed sentence on you
before the verdict was reached.
You cannot count on defense
in this burning world.
Hate's torch stares
into your dying eyes.

You are alone like rocks
in a dying tide.
Learn at last where you belong.
Go home in spirit,
then in flesh. Uproot yourself
from this vast ocean of hate.
You reaped nothing but the blows
of stormy seas.
If you must die, for G-d's sake
die at home where every pebble
preserves your father's blood.

ELEAZAR

Where shall we find strength
for this long voyage?
How can we fight with broken limb
and spine? Who will lead us
home to the ancient land? Answer me
that, oh great spirit of mine.

SPIRIT

While I stood before the curtain
I did not wait for any miracle.
But then this moment in time came
along and your broken words
forced me to act.
If now I return to your soul,
the eternal light of unseen passions
will become the new guide
of your fate.
Do you not see that I, the soul live
beyond the forms of flesh.
Have faith now as never before,
while your eyes witness night.

POPE

To me it seems past doubt
these prisoners
deserve death.

51

	Step forth now your last accuser.
SS OFFICER	I stand here on behalf of hell to charge them and the church as well.
POPE	(surprised) The church is not accused. You may only charge the prisoners. What does the nether world accuse?
SS OFFICER	The charge we bring is the same as your church has taught for centuries.
POPE	Then we may yet see eye to eye.
SS OFFICER	In this trial you cannot be judge, only witness. Leave your throne. I shall now take over.
POPE	If I may ask, in the name of what right?
SS OFFICER	In the name of Roman law which taught it is the right of the strong to break the weak. Your time is up. I demand your throne.

POPE
We protest: that all shall know,
only faced with naked force
we give up our throne.

The pope leaves the throne and sits in the place of the accusers. But in the gathering darkness all the accusers are disappearing and only the SS officer can be seen on the throne, and the accused. The SS officer stands up, with a Hitler salute.

SS OFFICER
Open earth, swallow
the world. Devils
of the nether world,
support us. Universe
be cleansed, for love
is dead. Wotan, mighty
spirit, come with us.

Now the pagans appear and their shadows sway fearfully in the dark. They all wear SS uniforms and the devil's face.

CHORUS
Wotan, Wotan, mighty spirit
come with us. We bit

out the tombs
of maidens wombs.

We stepped on infants in our boots.
We tore out scrotums from the roots.

And of them made
deadly nightshades.

Fathers, mothers we desecrated,
with their blood were satiated.

We broke up the gold
teeth from mouths of dead and old.

We turned the world to flame.
We shat the name

of God into the latrine.
The trees bled green.

We are bigger than all
the spirits. We rule over all.

We are deeper than the deep,
higher than the mountain steep.

We showed the world of men
the world's true face. Amen.

Kill kill kill
kill until
no life remains to spill.

The torture-chamber changes into a gas-chamber by means of
a shower descending. Incredible flames of the crematoria can
be seen. All the Jews and Spirit and girl are in it.

| SS OFFICER | You are in my power. |
| | Death trembles in your eyes. |

| SS OFFICER | |
| & CHORUS | Death, death, death, death. |

SS OFFICER	Poison gas will burst
	your lungs open. Night
	will deposit your ashes
	in the skies. And the wind

will carry the smell
of the burned bodies
into space,
where cold negation cries.

SS OFFICER
& CHORUS   And by tomorrow
                        when the sun awakes
                        not even the rags
                        of memory
                        will remain.

The chorus, like demented witches, dance around the Jews.

CHORUS   White is black
                        and black is white.
                        Death alone
                        cries in the night.
                        Blood tastes good.
                        To bite is bliss.
                        Long live Wotan's
                        eternal kiss.
                        Long live rape,
                        long live man,
                        the wretched ape.
                        Long live death,
                        eternal night,
                        where is God
                        and His Godly might?

While the devils dance around, repeating the verse quietly in
the background, the Spirit speaks.

SPIRIT   Never forget how things began,
                        the command of Sinai
                        and your deathless end.

Remember Masada and keep the vow
you took together then and now

that never again will you die as slaves.
Do not forget the waves

of hatred, and the ancient dreams.
Remember the hills, the ancient
plains and streams,

the pledge of your God
that you are His people
in this world.

While gas drizzles death in the nights
drink in the citrus scent
on Judea's heights.

In the blue skies the seabird
soars and weaves.
Behold the beauty of the
autumn leaves.

And in the ocean the fishes dance
as if in a trance.

A thousand winter deaths will be
your fate
on the shores of the Dead Sea.

But you will still be alive
in springtime.
The chimney smoke will climb

down, weary, at dawn and

you will attain your dream,
your home, your land.

The SS devils carry on dancing but like a film in slow motion
their movements are becoming slower and slower. And then
their shadows begin to fall apart. Everyone seems to be dead
except the Spirit, who stands like a statue over the seemingly
dead bodies. Then the Spirit and the girl cannot be seen any
more. Only the dead bodies are lying there. One can just see
in the semi-darkness a desolated courtroom and the chimneys
of the crematoria and further, somewhere like in the first
scene, the burning Masada. Dead silence; and then very
slowly (like in the ballet) the Jews stand up and in an eerie
fashion begin to move towards the audience. Peculiar lights
fall on the faces of these dead men. Eventually with their
white faces they just stand opposite the audience and slowly,
accusingly, lift their arms towards them.

PROLOGUE TO SCENE 6

SPIRIT

This is the last time
I face you here. The final scene
is about to start.
My spirit will be carried on
by those who build the land.
The land is more than soil, water, tree.
It is not merely space and maps
and miles
but all the centuries have accumulated.
I am the land.
When reality emerges
from the dream
the gentle veil of knowing
hides the past. How often
he whose face created

wonders,
stands before those wonders,
unbelieving.

SCENE 6

Ruins of the synagogue in Masada. Further down, fires are
burning. Smoke looms in the synagogue. Eleazar stands
amidst the ruins. Smoke whirling around his body. Beyond
the collapsed walls, one can see the mirror of the Dead Sea
and some remaining parts of the citadel of Masada. Eleazar is
clothed exactly as in the second scene. Dead bodies are
everywhere and he is talking to the Spirit.

ELEAZAR   Here the dream begins and here it ends.

SPIRIT   The dream's end often heralds dawn.

ELEAZAR   Cinders, a ruined shrine, death
                   and solitude as far as the eye can see.

SPIRIT   The sky's rim is not yet streaked
                   with purple. Maybe
                   the fiery dreams encircle you still.

ELEAZAR   (listens into the night)
                   Do I hear right? It seems the valleys
                   and the peaks are singing.
                   Who but the conquerors would sing?

SPIRIT   But listen, this is not the song of Rome.

Fragments of Hebrew melody and shouts of triumph rise from
the valley.

ELEAZAR	(agitated) The tattered words appear familiar. My heart recalls their lilt. Eternal Spirit, what is stirring? Victory?
SPIRIT	Yes, the sounds you hear mean triumph
ELEAZAR	(unbelieving) And Rome has passed away?
SPIRIT	And Rome has passed away.
ELEAZAR	(even more agitated) How could we triumph without an army? In God's name tell me: who defeated Rome's proud legions?
SPIRIT	Time and history. What you hear resounds from a new epoch. Israel is free again, and the land which knew such suffering, is once again your own.
ELEAZAR	What is dream? What is truth? O Spirit of God tell me, tell me now.
SPIRIT	Your dream is truth and your truth is dream.
ELEAZAR	Poison gas caught at my throat a moment ago. And before that, the crosses dripped with blood on these mountain peaks.

And Rome. And Silva.
And our thousand self-inflicted deaths.
And Sinai's vow
that death shall not prevail.
Help me, Spirit, in this dizzy whirl.
Who is the victor? Who is overcome?
And how can I hear the future sing?

SPIRIT   Man's world contains
   past, present, future.
Yet there are places, lives, fates
in the hands of God Almighty
that transcend time's barriers.
You, Eleazar, on old Masada, scan
the future, and your victorious sons
from their today
look back upon their past.

Eleazar falls on his knees.

Today your state
has been declared anew.

Eleazar bows his head.

ELEAZAR   So our death on this mountain
was not in vain?

SPIRIT   Your death, Eleazar, is ahead of you.
The question of death and life
will be in the hands of the sons
you now behold.
It is they who may make you proud.
It is they who may make you cry.

60

Akiva, Yehoshua and John come onto the stage, dressed as kibbutzniks. They have guns on them. They look towards Eleazar but cannot see him. They haul their flag up.

AKIVA,
YEHOSHUA
& JOHN

We sons of the old new land
pledge upon this mountain peak
before the eyes of past and future:
Masada lives, and shall always live
while your spirit
still flares in our souls.
Your death is an everlasting torch.
We vow upon this tragic peak
never to bear the world's contempt.
We swear to you, sages of old,
never to bear the yoke again
or place it on someone else's neck.

ELEAZAR

My Eternal God, thank You for this awakening,
for life, for death.

SPIRIT

(to all four)
Never forget:
the Idea triggers wonders,
moves centuries, sifts death, sifts life,
and has brought your people home
again.

ELEAZAR

Now this mighty miracle is done,
whither now, my God? I beg You,
tell me what is the goal?
Where is this Judean wind blowing?

Suddenly a tremendous storm crosses the sky. The Spirit falls prostrate on the ground, as do all the Jews.

VOICE   This is your truth:
                                doubt and faith together.
                                Uncertainly is your only certitude.
                                Death and life together are the truth
                                like two sides of a coin named destiny.
                                There is no start, no end,
                                only continuance and no solutions
                                within the bond of flesh.
                                Yet pain and death will teach you
                                secret words
                                and the dreadful truth hidden within
                                your soul.
                                Be not afraid of fear. But trust.
                                Faith is no mirage. Die now.
                                And come to life again.
                                Seek, search, suffer.
                                And then rejoice. This is your fate
                                as long as the earth revolves in space.

(Very low, echoing through the theatre)

                                Step out of time and return
                                to your todays before life's spark
                                fades into endless night.
                                Complete your voyage across
                                the somber years
                                and you will find answers
                                to your human plight.

As the Voice fades we are back in Scene 2. Only the burning synagogue is visible. Eleazar, dazed, gets up from the ground and then as one who understands where he is and what has happened, he slowly lifts his dagger. Where earlier the three

62

kibbutzniks stood now corpses are lying. Masada's corpses. Slowly Eleazar walks over, recognizing his daughter among the dead, hugs her to himself then buries the dagger in his own heart and falls down dead. Now only the fires are burning and crackling. The Spirit too has disappeared. For a few more moments there is silence, then Roman voices are heard.

Silva, Vetiliamus and seven Roman soldiers (the pagans) rush onto the stage. They stand alarmed before the dead. After a while Vetiliamus speaks.

VETILIAMUS General,
        everyone here is dead.

SILVA   (very slowly)
        That's what you think.

THE END

BIOGRAPHY OF THE AUTHOR EUGENE HEIMLER

Eugene Heimler was born on 27 March 1922 in Szombathely, Hungary, the son of a lawyer and prominent member of the Social Democratic Party. He became a successful poet in Hungary, with two volumes of poetry published before he was twenty. At age twenty-two, he was deported to Auschwitz, Tröglitz, Berga-Elster and Buchenwald. His beloved mother had died after a long illness shortly before the start of World War II. His wife Eva, his father, sister and her young son were murdered in Auschwitz. In 1946 Heimler married his second cousin, Lily, and in 1947 they immigrated to England. Soon after Dr Heimler received his diploma as the first psychiatric social worker from Manchester University, he began to develop his own social-integrative method, which became well known in Europe, America, Canada, South Africa and Australia under the name of the Heimler Method of Social Functioning (www.heimler-international.com).

Starting in the 1970s, he regularly returned to Germany in order to teach young Germans his unique approach in which frustration and suffering are used as potential for satisfaction and creativity, and as the means to find purpose and meaning in life. He became a consultant to the Ministry of Social Security in England, the World Health Organization and the government of the United States of America. For twenty years he taught his subject at the University of London, England and his fame led to chairs at several universities in the USA and Canada.

In 1984 his wife Lily died, leaving him two children.

In 1985 Heimler received an honorary doctorate from the University of Calgary, Canada, where he had taught his subject for seventeen years.

On the day marking the fortieth anniversary of the end of the war in Europe, he married Miriam Bracha, with whom he spent the last, very happy and fulfilled years of his life. Heimler died on 4 December 1990.

Heimler's work is being continued by practitioners in the Heimler Method and researchers around the world. His book *Night of the Mist* is a recognized Holocaust classic. His subsequent books – among them *Survival in Society, A Link in the Chain, The Healing Echo and Messages: A Survivor's Letter to a Young German* – also became well known internationally. Book descriptions can be found on www.newholocaustliterature.com. All his books are available on amazon.com.

Publications by Eugene Heimler

Now available at Amazon.com

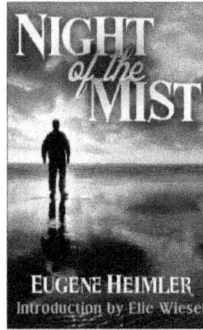

Night of the Mist
REVIEWS

Rabbi Dr. André Ungar

"Over half a century has passed since the events described in *NIGHT OF THE MIST*.

It has been over two decades since Eugene Heimler's own death in London on a cold, grey winter's day. But the story he tells is vividly, immortally alive. It is a tale of horror and heartbreak, of loss and degradation – yet also of hope and faith and warmth and humor and immortal humanity. It is unlike any other work that came out of the ashes of World War Two. His is a poet's voice as well as a philosopher's and a psychologist's. It is a young voice, an ageless voice. Our lives are the fuller for listening to it. ...It is a human document of great value. It contains wounds, both familiar and less familiar, that will long haunt the reader."

Elie Wiesel

"Eugene was 21 when he arrived at Birkenau. His description of what he saw, heard and lived through is sincere and restrained. He tells wonderful and moving stories of his childhood and adolescence in Hungary – his first loves and youthful reveries – the sudden German occupation – the wedding in the ghetto. The beginnings of fear, the intimations of the trials to come. The rebellion against destiny: Eugene and his loved one are married, but their happiness lasts only one night. Their honeymoon is spent in a sealed boxcar heading towards the unknown.

This gripping account is profoundly honest. The astounding episodes he relates are both atrocious and bizarre. In Auschwitz, a few paces from the crematoriums, the daughter of the chief of a Gypsy camp takes a liking to him. She feeds and protects him. They make love. In Auschwitz. Later on, *a Lagerältester* [head of the camp] takes notice of him. Thanks to an SS officer, he is put in charge of a group of ten young prisoners. Surely a guardian angel is watching over him. On the edge of despair, a man consoles him; it is the rabbi who officiated at his marriage so many eternities ago."

"These miraculous moments were more often than not engulfed in the all-encompassing climate of brutality. Heimler captures it well. The stark dehumanization of some, the desperate solidarity of others. The pangs of hunger: the power of attraction of a piece of bread. The disappearance of all traces of civilization, culture, morality. The conversations about the past, meditations on God, the dreams that make waking harder, more unbearable."

Professor Dr. Sarah Fraiman-Morris

"As a University professor who has been teaching literature of the Holocaust, I have read a lot of books on

67

this subject. I found that I could not put down this book; it was so captivating and well written. It qualifies as literature, since the author manages to tell the reader many things between the lines, just hinting and thus striking a cord in the reader's heart. The most unexpected things happen in this book.... The author's sensitivity, common sense, intelligence, modesty and warmth vibrate through the pages of this outstanding book, which I personally prefer to famous texts on the Holocaust such as for example Elie Wiesel's "Night". You will love this book!"

Mrs. Sheila Lyons

Eugene Heimler's memorable account of the holocaust is a work of the utmost poignancy and importance. This is a book which the adult reader will find difficult to put down. His descriptive narrative of the sufferings of those he lived with in the Concentration Camps during World War II - and his own fight for life - his inner growth and understanding, are quite exceptional.

The book takes on for the reader, a personal involvement in the brutalities, bestialities and horrors perpetrated on the inmates. That which would be unspeakable, Eugene Heimler has been able to articulate. The breakdown of all moral and ethical values, be they of the imprisoned or be they of their captors - a so called 'civilization' within a 'civilization'. It is quite extraordinary how Heimler makes this come to life. It is even possible to laugh at some of the incidents related; we can really see the funny side!

The portrayal of his own inner growth, his little acts of kindness albeit in an environment of unspeakable horror, his strength of character leaves the reader with a feeling that there's hope for us yet!

This small volume is a masterly account of man's inhumanity to man. A must for every student of Holocaust Studies and might I add, for every student of Political and

Social Studies.

"A dramatic and readable book."
The Times Literary Supplement

"Behind the eerie, the manic, the disgusting, he still conveys the desirability of life, the variety of human behavior, the power of imagination. His own conclusions were not of hate, but of discriminating tolerance."
Peter Vansittart in The Observer (London, England)

"This book deserves a place of its own in the literature of Nazi horrors, as it deals with those events from an unusual aspect – the effect of them upon the victims themselves."
Lord Russell of Liverpool

"There is no self-pity in Heimler's writing; just wonder at man's inhumanity to man … the massage he brings is not one of horror but of hope; of a fight back to life, and a life well worth living."
The Huddersfield Examiner

"This book has an important lesson to teach – that faith in God and in the dignity of man can overcome the greater evils that men can devise."
The Catholic Times

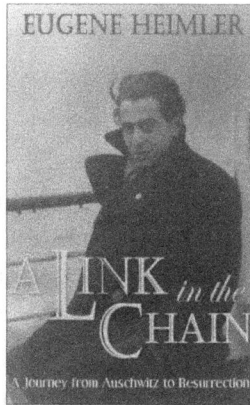

EUGENE HEIMLER

A LINK in the CHAIN

A Journey from Auschwitz to Resurrection

A Link in the Chain
A Journey from Auschwitz to Resurrection

In this second powerfully written volume of Eugene Heimler's incredible life's journey from a persecuted Jewish child in a small town in Hungary to world-renowned writer, therapist and teacher, Heimler is on his way home to Hungary from the concentration camps of Germany, where he had lost all his family. On this journey he experiences many life-threatening moments: being on a train with a former German SS man; witnessing the brutal rape of his traveling companion by Russian thugs; attempts on his life and being arrested and charged with treason in Hungary.

Eventually he reaches England and remarries, but his trials are manifold. After hearing that the Secret Police are torturing his friends in Budapest, he realizes he can never return to Hungary and has a breakdown. When a psycho-analysis helps him come back to life and regain his hope for the future, he is ready to act on an early ambition to become a writer and psychologist. He starts to write *NIGHT OF THE MIST,* which has become a world classic, and becomes a Psychiatric Social Worker. These challenges have their obstacles as well, and Heimler vividly describes his work as a Psychiatric Social Worker, including his refusal to give up on others—and himself. His experiences eventually lead to the development of a new method of therapy, which is today known as the *Heimler Method of Social Functioning*.

Throughout his life, Heimler consistently fought to help victims gain the courage to become victors. In *A LINK IN THE CHAIN* he once more tells his stories poetically and vividly.

Messages

A Survivor's Letter to a Young German

Eugene Heimler

MESSAGES

A Survivor's Letter to a Young German

Eugene Heimler, in his captivatingly poetic style, takes you with him on a life-transforming journey through seas of imagination and rivers of tears; from storms of pain to pools of individual and communal wisdom as well as deep inside his self and yours.

His universal and autobiographical stories, like the vivid colors on the canvas of a water-color artist, flow and dynamically blend time dimensions into an expanding, cohesive whole.

The diversity of genre, time and metaphor is startling and reveals multiple layers of our physical, emotional and spiritual reality.

The author transcends time as he interweaves past, present and future into a tapestry of deep meaning and passion, stained by blood and marked by tears and joy.

This book is about the author's journey of losing, searching and re-finding his own identity and place in his physical, emotional and spiritual worlds.

In his 'stream of consciousness' musings Heimler crosses time from biblical through medieval to modern human experiences of transformation through pain to self-discovery.

This artful intimate intertwining of personal, particular and universal themes draws the reader into Heimler's awe-inspiring multi-layered world of courageous introspection.

Messages illuminates how Heimler, as a Holocaust survivor, struggles to re-discover meaning, purpose and passion from his once shattered world.

Working through these challenges leads him to existential questions about the very meaning of life:

What are the connections between life and what we call death?

How can meaning transcend suffering?

How can we find peace if we deny our worst hours?

How can we understand all the hatred that surrounds us?

How can hate be turned into creativity instead of self-destructiveness?

What can keep our love and our ability to love alive in the midst of atrocities or indifference?

Come, join this remarkable man in his quest for eternal wisdom!

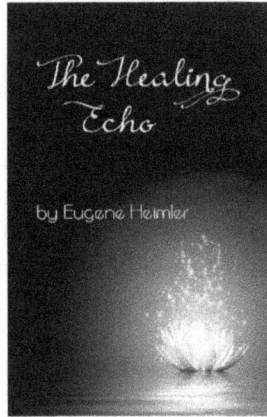

The Healing Echo

When Dr. Sigmund Freud's concepts and ideas penetrated Eugene Heimler's young Hungarian mind, the earth began spinning faster and lightening crossed the Western sky.

Two ingenious minds were crossing up there in the heights; both listened with respect – and then went their opposite ways: one to analysis, and the other to synthesis.

Eugene Heimler's pioneering philosophy, that our potential lies in the creative transformation of our negative forces, is as new a thinking in our 21st century as it was in the 1950s when it first broke ground. Heimler's radical idea that we need to harness frustration in order to flourish crossed the worlds of the post-industrial revolution and unemployment to our current age in which people search for the elusive meaningfulness of life.

The author had a 'paradoxical' title ready for his book: "The Gift of Unemployment", however, there was fear that hopeless 'victims' of unemployment would smash the shop-windows of book-sellers in Great Britain.

Yet, he, as well as those men and women whom he helped find meaning and purpose in their often shattered lives, was convinced, that his method works.

Not only people who are stagnated in their growth, but also children in kinder- gardens and schools can, with the help of Heimler's new approach, explore their untapped potential.

By listening to our inner selves, we can hear our echo, our echo that heals us and that helps us to live a fuller and happier life, to survive and thrive in our complex society. Eugene Heimler first echoed these thought in his ground-breaking book *"Survival in Society"*.

Now, by immersing yourself in *The Healing Echo,* you have an opportunity to enter this hopeful world of yet unimagined possibilities.

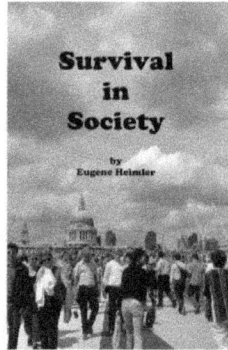

Survival in Society

Eugene Heimler's self-help method of social functioning has been developed and tested – and proven extraordinarily successful – for over forty years. Here he describes in detailed theory and through cases his interviewing and therapeutic techniques, in which a relationship of equality between 'helper' and 'helped' is paramount.

His aim has been to help people as individuals and in groups to make the most of their abilities, however latent, and to positively use their inner resources and past experience. He sees not only the past as influencing the present but present actions determining what we select from the past. Success or failure to function within ourselves and in society depends on the balance between satisfaction, defined as the ability to use one's potential, and frustration, defined as one's inability to use it. Too little frustration can be as damaging as too much: to function normally we constantly transform frustration into satisfaction. In other words, success is one's ability to transform the unacceptable – to oneself and to society – into the acceptable.

Throughout the book emphasis is placed on the importance for the individual of making his own decisions. Here he is helped by Heimler's decision-making tool – his *Scale of Social Functioning* – which enables him to understand his life situation and to act accordingly. The scale is of diagnostic value to the therapist, but its main use is to the patient.

Professor Heimler's method has been applied both to people in need of treatment and to 'healthy' individuals who want to explore their untapped potentials. It has been used by teachers at all educational levels to help students become more creative, in the employer/employee relationship, and by social workers in all fields. Heimler owes much to many past and contemporary practitioners. The originality of his work lies in his synthesis of existing theories and practices into a successful working method.

Now available at Amazon.com

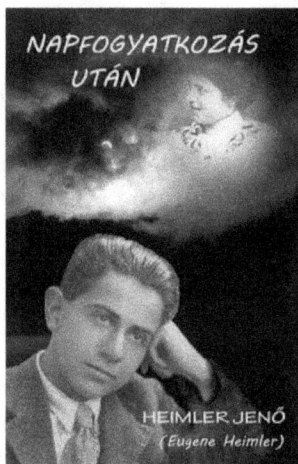

Napfogyatkozás Után

"***NAPFOGYATKOZÁS UTÁN***" is a publication of early poetry in Hungarian. It is a tribute to Eugene Heimler, whose poems had first been published weekly in newspapers in Szombathely when he was seventeen and were published under his pen-name "Vát Jenö" in three separate volumes between 1939 and 1946. Heimler defied his professors of Hungarian literature, who, about the time he wrote and published his poems failed him in Hungarian literature because he was a Jew and because of his revolutionary ideas. These men were fascists! The publisher, who after initial assistance terminated his contract, practically threw him out into the streets without any livelihood.

Antisemitism was very much alive and growing in Hungary.

78

How does one become a poet?
In his book "A Link in the Chain" Eugene Heimler writes:
"...My mother wanted me to become a poet when I was a child. I sat on her lap one winter evening, and she told me that this was her secret wish ..."
"...When I was nine years old, and mother was lying in bed with the illness that killed her in the end ... I was frightened that she might die, ... and sat down to write the first poem of my life... It was about a just king of Hungary, King Matthias. I waited until she woke, then I sat on her bed and read it to her. 'It's beautiful, Jancsi ... You are a poet all right ...'"
"... When I was fourteen years old, I sat one winter night alone in my little room while doctors fought for mother's life ... and ... I sat down then and wrote a poem for her. ...While I wrote, my tears fell on the ink ... the past was gone, and the good old days ... and mother might die ... tonight ... tomorrow ... or in a year's time? Before the specialist came next day ..., I read this poem to her, and said: 'You promised me once that you would recite my poems one day ...'. And to my father's surprise, she sat up in bed with tears in her eyes and recited the poem to us. I knew then that I should have to write, write a lot, to make her well. But she died when I was seventeen."
"... She was so happy when I wrote something. Ever since she died I always feel her presence when I have the pen in my hand."
"... I was so much attached to her, that I have been living a long secret winter night with her ... I have lived with her night and day, sitting in her lap long after she died."

[Publisher's Note:
In 2013 a memorial plaque was put up on the house of 11, Kings Street, Szombathely, Hungary, where the Heimler family had lived, commemorating Heimler Jenö.]

For further information on Dr. Eugene Heimler's life, books, philosophy and method of social functioning, please see
www.heimler-international.com
www.newholocaustliterature.com
Contact: Mrs. Miriam B. Heimler at mheimler1@gmail.com

BIOGRAPHY OF THE TRANSLATOR
ANTHONY RUDOLF

Anthony Rudolf was born 1942 and lives in London.

His <u>Translations</u> include:

Selected Poems of Yves Bonnefoy

The Soup Complex, a play by Ana Novac

Tyorkin and the Stovemakers
(selected verse and prose of Alexander Tvardovsky)

Boxes, Stairs and Whistle Time
(poems of Petru Popescu
Co-translated with the author)

The War is Over
(selected poems of Evgeni Vinokurov)

Selected Poems of Edmond Jabes

Other translations of many poets and prose-writers have been
published in anthologies and magazines.

Book of Poems
"The Same River Twice"

Poems, book-reviews, articles, stories, interviews, etc. were
published in numerous periodicals.

In the 1970's Anthony Rudolf acted as Managing- and
Literary Editor of European Judaism, Advisory Editor of
Heimler Foundation Newsletter and Modern Poetry in

Translation. He also was the London editor and distributor of Stand and the Founder and Co-Director of The Menard Press.

In addition he was the Guest-Editor of
Cambridge Opinion / Circuit (on language)
Workshop (Poetry translation issue)
Poetry Review (co-ed with Martin Booth)
Modern Poetry in Translation (French anthology)
New Linguist (poetry in translation)
Books National Book League (on the Jewish theme)
Roy Rogers, New York (European one-line poem section)

He also introduced Poems for Shakespeare IV
(Globe Playhouse Trust Publications) 1976
and co-edited (with Richard Burns) An Octave for Paz, which was published at Menard and Sceptre in 1973.

PUBLISHED BY THE MENARD PRESS:
- *Drypoints of the Hasidim* by F.T. Prince
- *Shema: The Poems of Primo Levi* (translated by Ruth Feldman and Brian Swann
- *Midrashim: Collected Jewish Parables* by Howard Schwartz

For full details of all books in print and forthcoming write to:

The Menard Press
8, The Oaks
Woodside Avenue
London N12 8AR
United Kingdom
e-mail: anthony.rudolf@menardpress.co.uk

For further information on Dr. Eugene Heimler's life, books, philosophy and method of social functioning, please see
www.heimler-international.com
www.newholocaustliterature.com

Contact: Mrs. Miriam B. Heimler at mheimler1@gmail.com

www.ingramcontent.com/pod-product-compliance
Lightning Source LLC
Chambersburg PA
CBHW020513030426
42337CB00011B/359

* 9 7 8 0 9 9 8 9 5 9 3 1 3 *